The Old Flea-Pit

By the same author

Poems
The Railings
The Lions' Mouths
Sandgrains on a Tray
Warrior's Career
A Song of Good Life
A Night in the Gazebo
Collected Poems 1952–83

For Children
To Clear the River (*as John Berrington*)
Brownjohn's Beasts

With Sandy Brownjohn
Meet and Write 1, 2 and 3

As Editor
First I Say This
New Poems 1970–71 (with Seamus Heaney and Jon Stallworthy)
New Poetry 3 (with Maureen Duffy)

Criticism
Philip Larkin

Translation
Torquato Tasso (from Goethe)

Signed for Audrey Green —

The Old Flea-Pit

Alan Brownjohn

— all good wishes —

Alan Brownjohn
Thornbury Festival
12th April 1991

HUTCHINSON
London   Melbourne   Auckland   Johannesburg

This edition first published in 1987 by Hutchinson Ltd,
an imprint of Century Hutchinson Ltd,
Brookmount House, 62–65 Chandos Place, London, WC2N 4NW

Century Hutchinson Australia Pty Ltd,
PO Box 496, 16–22 Church Street, Hawthorn, Victoria 3122, Australia

Century Hutchinson New Zealand Limited,
PO Box 40-086, Glenfield, Auckland 10, New Zealand

Century Hutchinson South Africa Pty Ltd,
PO Box 337, Bergvlei, 2012 South Africa

Photoset by Rowland Phototypesetting Ltd,
Bury St Edmunds, Suffolk

Printed in Great Britain by
The Guernsey Press Co. Ltd,
Guernsey, Channel Islands

British Library Cataloguing in Publication Data

Brownjohn, Alan
   The Old Flea pit.
   I. Title
   821'.914   PR6052.R62

   ISBN 0-09-168271-1

For the Areopagus

Acknowledgements

are due to the following, in which these poems, or versions of them, have previously appeared: *Agenda*, *Ambit*, *Arvon Postcards*, *BBC English*, *Encounter*, *Graffiti*, *Hubbub*, *The Literary Review*, *The London Magazine*, *The London Review of Books*, *New Poetry 7*, *The New Statesman*, *Poems for Poetry '84*, *Poetry Australia*, *Poetry Book Society Supplements 1980*, *1983*, *1984*, *1985*, *1986*, *The Observer*, *Outposts*, *The Spectator*, *Thames Poetry*, *The Times Literary Supplement*, *Voices from Arts for Labour*, *A Winchester Folio*, *With a Poet's Eye*.

Contents

Continuation

Now suddenly noticed, a little way ahead,
The figure stands in the middle of the road
Not moving apparently, its back turned,
Its arms out of sight.

                  And this is daylight,
So I smile at feeling all the more disturbed,
And at wanting to prove that it must be harmless.

I shall walk so as to be heard inside the hood
The figure wears, not to scare it in turn
By approaching too quickly from behind;
And set my feet more deliberately down
On the frosty ground, tap my stick more distinctly.
When I glance up for the comfort of the sun,
A seabird flies and cries over the blue,
Neck stretched in anguish . . .

                  She or he might be ill,
And fixed in this rigidity by some thought
Too terrible to confront or to speak out.
There is a woman in the way it stands,
And a question of what words ought to be said.
Will she require to be coaxed back carefully,
And seen to her gate and doorway, and left
With a clumsy sense of some duty half-performed?
– Then brooded over in the coming days,
Whenever I pass the curtains which never move,
And the darkness behind them after dark?

. . . I have overtaken her now, and catch
A face alive enough, but raw and frozen,
Which turns as mine turns, to acknowledge me;
But her eyes go frowning back to an open book:
One hand grips its spine, while the other writes
Black line after line of writing, covering all
The space on every leaf, she is half-way
To filling it.

In the seconds as I pass,
She has seen that I have seen it, so we both smile;
But nothing is asked or given, nothing spoken,
Except a glance to recognize that we heard
And saw one another, and were not surprised,
And had rendered ourselves both natural after all,
To a road, and a winter afternoon.
                                   She frowns;
And writes. We continue as we were.

Looking at Her

When he looked at her, he invariably felt
Like stretching his arms up, as if about to do
A long and lustrous yawn. Of course she knew
She had that effect; and whether she lounged or knelt,
Or walked or simply stood, he was never clear
If she was prepared and eager to let him bring
His hands down around her neck, and press her near
– Or would shake her head and permit him no such thing.

This was her talent, to stir both lust and doubt,
She did it the best of all feats she was able;
And therefore other women felt sure she bored
The men she attracted; since all of them, without
Her seeming to provoke them, of one accord
Would yawn and thump their fists down on the table.

Still Small

Does your walk have to go in a great circle?
That looks like craving novelty to the last,
Or dreading to revisit a recent past
Which instantly became non-viable.

– Whereas to march forward, halt, and swivel round
About three or four steps from the top of the hill
Would show a fantastic strength of will . . .
And all the excitements of unknown ground

– The greenhouse, the granary – would still be there
For another day. So stop; and turn your face.
There are nicer things to see in the same place
When you travel back, e.g. you are now aware

That those are not gun-toting wildfowlers
Snarling in combat jackets under the trees,
But birdwatchers at their mild observances
Lifting innocuous binoculars

– And the land beyond the hill might obviously
Prove lack-lustre in the end. In the end,
Are the best things always round the next bend?
Might they not be what you passed and failed to see?

Turning back was the interesting thing to do!
You face the sunset with a stronger stride,
The contours surge you homeward like a tide,
The wind in the dark trees is cheering you.

Entering My Fifty-third Year

Another animal lounges on my table,
With none of my guilts or aspirations.
He has been poisoned with boiler-fumes, had
Ear-mites and eczema, undergone a short
Paralysis of his hindquarters and survived.
Last year he used up one of his lives in causing
A twenty-ton lorry to swerve into a ditch.
Have I done as much for the environment?
In a moment he will probably leave me
And go over to the garden of the Grapes,
Where people who do not know him from Adam
Will feed him with bacon scratchings and ploughman's cheese.
Would they do as much for me? They do it for him
Because he is definable, they know what he is
And the little things he likes. Today I am as many
Cards as there are in the pack and weeks in the year,
And they would not know where to have me: a merman
Stranded between the tempests of youth and the dried-up
Plateau of walking-frame and electric blanket.
If they found out, what would they make of seven books
Where the life not coded in poems is hidden in blurbs,
And a foot (of Achilles, or Oedipus?) twisted
On a Norwegian mountain and creasing me now
As I lope a birthday mile on a corrugated beach?
I crunch over empty shells in my swimming trunks,
Past forbidden nudists rejoicing in the comfort
That the undressed self may be itself and find
Great spiritual solutions and repose . . .
What is that, they might just ask? It has two legs
Quite suited to a kilt, up to the knees,
But beyond that only girth and ungainliness,
And not-of-the-newest. I limp, and ask myself
How much longer has this machine? It prolongs
Its life with meticulous arrangements, hating to leave
A chair not parallel with the table, or find
The Co-op coffee granules on the wrong shelf;

9

But it grows slower with its diligence.
It listens less and less when people answer
The questions it poses, they might not have been speaking.
The issues it sorely wants to understand
Might be happening elsewhere. Last night, having had
A dream of death, it groped downstairs and ravaged
The biscuits by torchlight at four a.m., as usual.
It hopes it works them off with exercise.
– Today I am still running after the slim one
Who was never there in the past, but some time might be,
Pursuing the true self in this trampled shell:
Inside a man half-a-stone too heavy is a man
So light, and lightheartedly serious, he really finds
Life is both profound and easy; not this tired struggle
In the effort to grasp the *scherzo con espressione*
Which the cat has played without trying all his days.

Profoundest Love

She gave him sand from the Tyrrhenian Sea,
He sent her a present of sand from the shores of Lake Erie.

He dropped some grains of her sand on the edge of the lake,
But kept the others, it helped him remember her.
She mingled a bit of his sand with the verge of the sea,
But retained some grains in a tiny box because
They reminded her of him.

And this was happening everywhere in the world,
Whole deserts exchanged between Asia and Africa,
And people everywhere swopping seedlings and saplings,
Whole forests exchanged between Finland and Brazil.

Cat-lovers transplanted whiskers from their cats:
'My cat has your cat's whisker and yours mine.'
We think of each other much more often that way.

I stood by the motorway watching the sand trucks pass,
I saw huge lorries transporting uprooted trees,
I saw vets' ambulances speeding with mad blue lights
– The whiskers for the transplants.
My name is Vladimir Nikolaich:
Back indoors I switch on a radio I cannot understand,
I am in High Wycombe, the news is in English here.
My Rosemary knows no Russian, I love her so much,
And she is in Kharkov switching on the radio
And comprehending nothing in the least

– Except that we exchanged for one another,
And think of each other very much indeed.
Ours was an act of the profoundest love.

Last Table

In a corner under a foreign calendar,
In the hot draught from the kitchen, is the last
Table: a dump for cruet stands and boats
Of *sauce tartare*. And spread across the stains
On its tablecloth is a folded noon edition
Scrawled on in red with ticks and question marks.
And here a chair with a much less brilliant
Back than the golden seats of customers
Contains a waiter, whose unbending grace
Showed, when he served, detachment from all food
As a doctor's manner may transcend disease.
Here he sits at one a.m. as you depart,
Here he sits alone, the bow tie sprawling loose,
And spoons up meat from a shallow, yellow bowl.

Waterloo Road

A last trump of the suburbs, the Elephant
Calls up its traffic from five directions
And debouches it on the City. Yet again
I swerve this dog-leg to confront the green
In the centre of St George's Circus
– On my Super Scale map of London it makes
The shape of Napoleon's hat. Here Waterloo Road
Begins its rainy stretch up to the river
Past garage, café, theatre, a grey half-mile
Slowing down to a darkness under the railway
Where pedestrians cross it and not notice.

It lends its commemorative name to a link
Between two roundabouts, it only wants
To shrug off all identity, collecting
Structures and spaces at random. Through
Its beggars' guts the age goes on a progress
Blasting them with its own indignities:
Dark suits perform in unseen offices;
Financial towers gloss over council benches
Where the feckless sit out programmed days;
Up at the Bridge the columns of St John's
Survive to appeal to deafened air.

I have survived this far, not met my own.
Up Waterloo Road I make my progress thinking
That Life is an undoubted victory,
Of the same kind as this. It renders you
A similar anonymous means of passage
From birth to death, one roundabout to the next.
It grants the age its progress through your head.
It lays at your feet the hats of conquerors
Reduced to a patch of inner-city grass.
All its stations end in greyness, exits onto
Passionless stretches where life must go on.

Box

It was really remarkable
You should ring after all these years . . .
I was on the brink of a quite
Momentous decision, I mean
A momentous *gaffe*, in my life;
And your call dragged me back from it
Like suddenly finding a room
Where I stood there at the window
And was just preparing to jump!

You cannot explain why you got
In touch? Well – *telepathy*, yes?
What else sent your hand racing out
To a telephone down in Strood
To release this bit of your past
Like a small, crated holy ghost
In Leeds? Your desire to explore
What things your past might be doing
By ringing it up was so *right*.

And there could be more out here, yes?
If you phoned me a second time?
Just dying for that little nudge
To enter the present and bring
New life – and old fascinations –
To a friend it recalled so well
(Who had clearly remembered *it*?)!
I am just like I was, you know,
Except this tiny bit older . . .

Aren't you awfully glad you rang?

In January

In the salt-marshes, under a near black
Sky of storm or twilight, the whole day
Dark on the creeks where the wind drives wavelets back
Against the filling tide, I have lost my way

On a path leading nowhere, my only guide
The light half-way up a television mast
Five miles across the waste; and if I tried,
I could imagine hearing, under this vast

Raw silence of reeds and waters, the deep drone
Of generators, gathering up the power
To send its message out; and, stopped alone
By this channel's edge, revisit a lost hour

At a restaurant table, in a vanished place
(An organ chiming in the hushed cave below)
When three sat smiling in an alcove space
And saw their futures, thirty years ago . . .

And ten years earlier, learn each adverb clause
Written out in the spring by those in dread
Of School Certificate; without much cause
For fearing death as long as they had read

The good green textbooks. Further back, next to me,
Her pencils in a leather pouch, her dress
A blur of gentle yellow, is a she
Who smiles with such a sidelong vividness

I can even touch her hand. And further still,
I walk up between desks rising in tiers,
And see the old imperial pictures fill
The walls of the same room, lit by gasoliers

– My father's now. Then suddenly return
To the path over the marshes, and the light
On the meccano mast, which tries to burn
As strongly as a fixed star, secure and bright

Against the black of nightfall; and provides
Small quizzes for our lounges, puppets that grin
To tame the evening's terrors. England hides
Its head in its small comforts . . . Seeing in

– Alone and lost and darkling – this New Year,
I stare round at the dark miles of this nation,
And through the winter silence only hear
The loveless droning of its generation.

Saturday Morning

I

Crossing the end of Lancaster Grove
Is the Chinese girl, looking back at her huge man;
And she does not see the Scirocco swinging round,
Does not even see it missing her,
Only hears him roar, with an anger tired
From telling her so many times before:
'Can't you watch where you're bloody going!'
She smiles to admit her inattention,
Or show her indifference. In the man's hand
A cat-basket swings about, in the basket,
Immune to all occasions, a ginger cat
Sits, bemused and sociable.

II

In another hour, I put down the telephone
And go out to buy some socks. 'Not short-
And-flimsy,' I say, '*or* long-and-rough.'
'So medium wool,' says Henry the outfitter,
Who can outfit anyone. 'Try these. – Yes, sir?'
Behind me: 'Have you any denim shoes?'
Asks Lindsay Anderson. 'Only these,' says Henry,
Who has left me for a second with the socks.
'Only *those*?' says Lindsay Anderson. 'The trouble is
One is getting so conservative.'
'We are,' says Henry with authority,
'Expecting some more in.'

Lieder
(for Peter Porter)

Horseman, horseman galloping with the wind! Look at me, look at me, I am the beautiful daughter of the King of the Hobgoblins. If you look at me but once I will gallop at your side, and lead you down, down into the caverns of the Hobgoblins.

The poet sings: Although I am forbidden your company, although you write me whole pages, whole books, whole libraries of cruel rejection, I shall still come and play my piccolo under your casement. Remember, only timid young ladies obey their mothers.

The young man says: You may think I am like a kite on your string, that I will obey every tug of your heartless fingers. Beware, beware! One day I shall refuse your bidding and flop down into the mud.

The poet sings: I love my cat, and I love you. My cat is small and warm, and so are you. My cat plays with me and has sharp claws, and so do you.

The young peasant is very lazy, but his beloved is very short in stature. I will take up my shears, he says, and cut and cut at the grass until I can see you, my dear. What wonders, O what wonders love will accomplish!

She says: If you are a butterfly, I shall be a net. If you are a rose, I shall be a pair of secateurs. If you are some crisps, I shall be a wrapper, and you will be ready salted. I am a most determined young woman.

The poet, starving and penniless, sings for the King. O what gifts, O what glories, says the King. They are worth more than all the banquets and all the gold in the world – and turns the poet out into the snow at the palace gate.

In a Restaurant

The facing mirrors showed two rooms
Which rhymed and balanced beautifully,
So everything we wore and ate
Shone doubly clear for you and me.

In the next image after that
Life seemed the same in every way:
Green bottles and white tablecloths
And cutlery as clean as day;

But in the third, things looked a mite
Less brilliant than in the first two . . .
A sort of mist was falling on
The features of a dwindling view,

And by the time our gaze had gone
Searching down to rooms eight and nine,
The world seemed darker, and confused,
Its outlines harder to define,

Its faces tinier. There, instead
Of warmth and clarity and bright
Colours for everything, we saw
A shadow land, a listless light

Which neither of us understood:
A place so closed and small and black
It nearly hurt, smiling, gripping
Our glasses harder, coming back.

A Fear of Wilderness

They leap without letting on they intend to,
These cats. Assuming they always do land
In amenable safety, they cling to
Your lap with four paws cold from the darkness.
You shiver at the ice they bring in them.

But slowly your legs regain a heat,
Their claws retract, and the vacillating tail
Has finished; the four feet now turning warm.
What had been once, outside the door, a fear
Of wilderness is now a comfortable

Interesting glow, of cities seen from trains
You are neither entering nor pausing in.
You pat and patronize, they settle down
To a steady breathing. In the yellowed light
The two of you are rational animals.

Dream

Once again driving along a motorway
To a reading perhaps, or on holiday;
But this time accompanied by the slim,
Much older figure of a woman nearly
Loved many years ago, now on a whim
Called up and taken out for a clearly
Mistaken trip into nostalgia: this
Doesn't work, our fifty-year-old kiss

Isn't much of a physical recollection . . .
We come to an A road, and an intersection
Gives us a kind of mini-roundabout,
A circular hump of concrete, hard and white,
With three roads to choose from; but we are in doubt
Which road is the correct one, and are quite
Surprised to see that a fourth road has been closed
By planting grass on it. Still, we have nosed

Into what we guess to be the proper
Route, and we do not pause to stop a
Passing pedestrian dressed in red to ask
If we *are* pursuing the right track,
Though all at once it becomes a tiresome task
Avoiding the bumps and ruts. We can't turn back,
The road is no more than a narrow, hedged-in lane,
'Unadopted' possibly? And again,

Though we doubt if we have hit upon the right
Direction, we drive on, jolting, until we sight
A long, low, disinfected building, obviously
A very modern hospital, because
As we step out and slam the doors we see
A vestibule, with chairs, and corridors
Down which cream-uniformed nurses disappear
With files or clipboards in their hands; and hear

The muzak seeping its reassurance:
Nothing to test our patience and endurance,
Just a slow, gleaming harmony. Not afraid,
We go aside into a clinical
Ante-room where there are sinks, and laid
On spotless surfaces a finical
Array of ambiguous instruments . . . Along
A wall on metal tables sit three strong

White-coated women, very unattractive,
And one of them starts forward, an active,
Smiling and businesslike blonde who is the friend
I drove with – she who travelled *with* me!
In her hand is a kind of textile ball, a blend
Of gauze and other fabrics. And I can see
It's shaped like a rather large contraceptive,
Or a pair of underpants. I'm not receptive

To what appears to be her wild-eyed, rare
Desire to try it on me, somehow, somewhere . . .
The other women watch, and shift their haunches
To have a better view from where they sit,
And I realize I am dreaming, as she launches
Into a menacing harangue – oh not one bit
Am I enjoying any of this, struck down
With revulsion in my seat. The women frown,

But of the three I note the pleasantest,
And then conclude that I must do my best
With this dream and the challenge it is making.
I shout, 'Let's have that horrible device!'
My friend smiles now, yet she is taking
That panti-web of gauze away, and twice
I grab for it, and only the third time snatch
And hold the thing, and with it run and catch

The nicest of these cold Eumenides,
Who lets herself be caught; and then I seize
Myself and wrap up in this bunched-up gauze,
And take her with it. So the others can
Now fade into a background of moaned applause
For what we do. Waking, I hear a van
Which drones a plaint of sighs and happy tears:
A burst of rock as it engages gears.

Even

Not a morning person, I as usual rose
At half-past eleven, the self-possessed hour,
A lord of the day's maturity, despising
Dawn's blatant desire to astonish
– Not guessing that the waters had risen too.

Yes, men had been out with hooters going round
On bicycles while I slept, warning the town
Of the fact of the brand-new cracks in the sea
Defences. I felt, at nine, I am fairly sure,
One infinitesimal shiver, though . . .

It hardly shook one leaf in the sleek trees
In the garden where I lay stretched out for years
Getting even with reality. It just felt
Unimportant. I slept on, dismissing it
As a small stir of automatic guilt.

Monday Morning

Sir, at the window of the study where
His prayer-books blocked the walls, grabbed for his bell
And the clapper was missing; so he shook
A silence at the playground. Many years
Before it could be technically so,
The sound had gone and left only the vision:

The vision of a bell vainly swinging
At a lordly wrist while our little world
Played on regardless of his stare. *Inside*,
Inside! he had to shout. And we all trooped
Inside to our places, mine being under
A secular picture somewhere near the back.

Picture the wind and rain in tantrums,
And me enjoying lovely hours of learning
In that school of life. Miss Wyke's bright-coloured chalks
Are poised at the blackboard writing truths, the room
Basks in a lime-green shade on sunny days
When the blind is down. And I feel my elbow

Nudging Miss Wyke's cool shoulder as she bends down
To read what I have written, all her red ticks
Fall lavishly across my splendid pages.
And then there come the long, long holidays,
All lustrous on lawn and sundial, where I wish
The shadow spun much faster than it did:

I am yearning for the shadow of Miss Wyke
To bring maturer wisdoms in September.
In my secret exercise-book I make
The summer hours more sweet, Miss Wyke draw near
By invoking her grace in fictions, in tales
Where I find the bell-notes are scarcely needed.

About this time I find inside myself
A social conscience in the shape of marbles
Cadged out of Barbara, who said she liked me.
They touch with glassy kisses and are gone,
And I mourn in the alley's red-and-white globe
The transience of gain, the truth of loss.

– Today I gained the top of the hill and saw
The school, in the haze of distance tinier
Than houses in Monopoly. Barbara
Could be the figure I picked up and set
On the doll's house swing in the recreation
Ground alongside. Night blotted out the scene,

A night in which I find Miss Wyke in dreams
Among her books and music, in Sir's room now.
She asks me to say sorry to Barbara,
And run life sensibly, without a bell.
The fields and towns I see in her unstained windows
Are much more like real worlds. I read her books.

Theatre

Oh look, a dog walking along by himself!
I can tell he wants me to believe he has
A destination.

When I dragged the curtains aside, they became
A fourth wall enclosing his performance of
A purpose, strolling

Across the stage of the street not sniffing, not
Diverted by anything. And see, a cat
Which connives at this

Dog's desire to seem busy, therefore just sits
And knows he will be safe. What fine perception!
The dog exits, left,

And he is now in the past, the cat and I
Have entered the present where nothing happens,
And three large blue cars

Driving past is not dramatic, only part
Of everyday life. Except that in that house
A curtain opens,

And a face cranes out with crude astonishment
At three glossy cars! They cross his empty stage,
They want him to think

They had a destination and a purpose,
And at the corner a policeman has connived
At their busy wish.

We might try hard, but this other face and I
Cannot see the same production. Entranced, he
Stands there gazing, but

For me events of tables and chairs inside
The room behind me are more amazing now.
Let the play go on

In the eye of this other beholder, I
Shall finish with it and pull my curtains, sad
At so many walls.

A View of Nowhere

Our long thin legs exaggerate our steps
As we prance and stalk up the dunes lugging huge
Transistors. We are mechanical toys
Wound up and pointed over nowhere, blue
Windcheaters, canvas shoes, obedient
Creatures who would not guess how much we *are*
Our elementary times. Did all those beards
And bowlers and high collars ever guess
How they posed for their own bourgeois age?

The old serene sun of late afternoon
Draws out our shadows. Suddenly you hear
Our music turning quaint, collectable,
And see our clothes draped on museum stands . . .
In a moment we ourselves will be gone too,
Along the sepia roads of this July,
Not guessing how the sea outlasts it all,
Pushing back at us today more signatures
Of what we are: torn sea-birds on our sand.

Watermark

The lovely Anita, in earrings already
At twelve, in the nineteen-forties, looks out today
Through a Speak Here perspex veil in a Barclay's Bank.
With her awesome self-possession, she was equal
To any approach; and strolled the – respectable – streets
Surrounded by gallants who furnished heavy aid
Against strangers who dared a look at one precious gilt lobe.

Our middle age should have altered a lot of things
– The shy boy level now with the beautiful doll,
One broke and the other plain. But where life's ledger
Builds columns of meticulous disenchantment,
Anita still sits tight at the clasp, making sure
That its cheques and balances add up to dead stop
On all extravagant longings; a tarnished bell
Calling gallant support against those who might grasp the gold.

Visitor

A slip road slopes off from the arterial road,
Running parallel to it for a bit,
Then veers inland and comes between two rows
Of passive terraced houses, fitted out
With concreted front gardens whose wooden gates
Will open to a thumb pressed on a latch.
A gate jars on one step, the letter box
Is clacked three times, as if this is arranged.
When she opens it, a banister offers
A post to drop a coat on, and there is heard
A cinema organ in the kitchen,
Braying a ballad on a wireless set.

The hall is tiny, and she makes a smile
Providing the back-facing sitting-room
Where, if the crimson curtains drew apart,
A line of dazzling washing, the purged wear
Of the past week, would slice the square of lawn
Diagonally into two triangles;
But as the sun is bright, the curtains hide it.
She moves as she is moved, where she is moved,
Half-stumbling downwards, falling sprawled across,
In cotton dress and apron, the settee
Below the biscuit barrel. Now the runner
On the sideboard shifts a fraction, being brushed.

It reaches five-and-twenty to eleven
On this quiet weekday, and the mid-morning post
Spreads a brief shade across the door . . . She stands
Out of sight to re-open it, and make
A quick farewell, and close it, and turn alone.
She turns towards the empty banister.
She wonders if it ever took place at all.
None of the furniture is stained or scratched,
The settee on its castors has not moved
As much as an inch. In a beam of the sun,
The dust still goes across and up and down
Behind her in the sitting-room. In the hall,

The letter on her mat is not picked up.
She thinks about stooping to pick it up,
Then knows she cannot stoop but only stand,
Stand shaking as she grips the banisters
So tightly that her trembled hands turn white
And her wrists go thin with the horror. No one will know.
Anything that was here is cleared away,
As surely as the stains on the clean clothes
Strung out on all the washing lines. As yet
There are no radio phone-ins she might try
Blurting the worst to, to be mollified
By solace from the airwaves. And besides,

She is not on the phone.

The Exit of Dr Fitzsimmon

In the seventeenth hour of the symposium
The trolley came slowly round the door.

The deconstruction of syllabuses paused
For the gathering up of cups.

Each one sublimed the lust for liberty
With a courteous device:

There were those who helped the lady by handing over
A teacup lopsidedly couched inside
Another one, in a spillage of grey tea.

And others pulled down sugar-bowls from ledges,
Or fingered spoons from between the legs of chairs.

But the Rev. Dr Fitzsimmon, as the dinner lady
Applied all her dutiful strength to the door to drag out

Her tiers of rattling crocks,
Leapt up to serve her, his papers stuffed
Unconsciously under his left arm.

And with his right arm Dr Fitzsimmon
– From the outer side, on the landing – held the door
Most graciously extended, so the lady and her cargo
Might trundle on through.

Cups and saucers gone,
The meeting went back to its dry labyrinth
With Dr Fitzsimmon gone, undoubtedly escorting

The dinner lady on through other doors
Further off down the long, long passages, swing doors, main doors,
But every one of them leading him ultimately on
To the great Front Door of the Polytechnic
And the Car Park beyond:

An ingenious man,
A chivalrous man,
A free and exultant man driving home to his wife

In his Renault 14.

Programme

'. . . take you to the medicine man. He got cures no white man ever
hear of.'

– from a horse opera

I insert the computed card in the lock of the door,
And press down the handle. And I'm inside.

Oh this is good: bed, table, telephone.
From here I could ring all the way to England,

I could telephone to someone with an *I Ching*,
And say, try it with toothpicks, give me some *truths*.

I tire of the columns on the concertina sheets;
There has to be more, much more, than the print-out tells.

Yes, how I need chance and magic, how I need luck,
How I need synchronicity. I see from here

In socialistic order, ranks and ranks
Of grey-eyed digits, explaining, explaining. Christ,

I need some cure for all my neat afflictions,
Astrology, theosophy, or just

Some pure, electric, archetypal thing to blow
All this regular world to fucking smithereens.

Before the Game

This is the coin
spinning in air
to decide who wins the toss.

This is the thumb that flicked the coin
spinning in air
to decide who wins the toss.

This is the hand that owns the thumb
that flicked the coin
spinning in air
to decide who wins the toss.

This is the brain that controls the hand
that owns the thumb
that flicked the coin
spinning in air
to decide who wins the toss.

And this, over here, is the twelfth man,
who lent the coin
as a method of being noticed for something
if not for his part in the game.

It is the custom here that the loser of the toss
keeps the coin as a consolation
for the brutality of Fate.

The owner of this coin did not know of the custom,
or he would not have lent for the purpose
a rare doubloon
of the Emperor Paronomasia IV.

As it spins, he watches it, trying to seem unaffected,
thinking, Will I ever get it back?

The situation is complicated by the fact
that the doubloons of the Emperor Paronomasia IV
have two heads.

Mares

The pink dog darts about on the edge of the sideboard.
The water rises eagerly to his feet.
It will fill the polished horn of the gramophone,
Submerging the strings of the salon orchestra
In their antique love song. The tenor is singing, 'Turn
The garden tap off, love, poor Spot will drown.'

Commander of a pirate underground train,
A prominent liberal journalist guides it
Up the tunnel. In the illumined coaches,
The passengers undress for hard-porn video
And electro-convulsions. On an escalator,
An inspector points and shouts, 'We'll get you, you bastard!'

Nothing wrong with the great capacious bed,
Or with the three schoolgirls all snuggling up;
And no jealousy of the smallest one, with glasses,
When I see her next morning by the fruit machine;
She is only cutting a loose thread off the sweater
Of a Pakistani nuclear physicist.

If I went a day earlier than I plan to,
They wouldn't shoot me on the hotel steps;
If I arranged another hotel altogether,
Or took an earlier flight, they still might not;
If I went by sea, not air, that might be safer.
All the hotels are my former Oxford college.

Petronella sidles up smiling to tell me
How the old flea-pit has suddenly re-opened,
A stone's throw from the crematorium.
We ought to queue early, I like Petronella,
Her lips are flecked with urticaria,
They love her at the crematorium.

A fabulous welcome: met at the station
By an orchestra of centaurs in dinner jackets.
'We'd like to give you the honour' – the first violin –
'Of conducting us in some items.' 'But I've never –'
'Oh yes you have!' – 'But I'm unable –' 'Please,
Here's the baton. You know *La Boutique Fantasque*.'

The woman has been working hard on relaxation
In front of the cameras. Against all custom,
She lights and draws on a black and white cigarette.
The smoke through her teeth fills up, blanks out, the screen.
We only hear an antique voice, proclaiming.
The water rises eagerly to her feet.

Nature Poem

An English landscape, a water-colour prairie
Where cattle crop in amiable herds

Looking free enough, but each one wanders
On somebody's leash, and few of us know whose,

Except I do know that the poles which race
To communicate with the farm on the horizon

Have leashed it to the city, even though I can't see
Their connecting wires with a naked eye,

Though the naked mind can connect them, the cattle fatten
On city-packaged feeds, the jolly farmer

Stands mimicking commercials which mimic him
In the Ploughman's Bar, the power relayed

From elsewhere dots today's essential screens
With agri-computations, all the data

Terminating there, where the farmer's boy
Now drums, a confident heel, on a keyboard

In his skyline office, the unleashed thought
Cropping powerlessly over the unhedged fields.

On My Recent Birthday

Yet another dentist chalks up a low opinion
Of my courage. I drive back between conifers
Up a lane past a pool where agile moorhens
Display the ability to walk, fly, paddle or dive.
The grown ones teach the young ones, or the young ones
Have it instinctively; but young humans
Will differ from their parents and disappoint them,
Displaying insouciance on the dentist's couch
When the family thing was cowardice; or vice versa.
This is our difference from the animals,
This tendency not to follow the family rules.
What father moorhen wins a Sandhurst sword
And lives to see his son retailing badges
To be worn by 'Bird-lovers Against the Bomb'?
The conifers drop their cones, plant life goes on
In a million pots and forests, following precedent
And nothing else at all. But the dentist's children
Slip through the teeth of their inheritance,
Make small unchippable moorhens in plasticine
In their pre-school playgroups. They cannot walk,
They cannot fly, or paddle, and under water
They stay down for ever. They have varied,
Like everything made by man, including man.

Performers

What starts as a flat sheet of card
Is folded, folded over, into a cube
And a flap left open: See, empty!
The flap has a tongue, slotted in
And the whole thing's closed. The performer

Pretends to be childishly fond of his box,
He shakes it and it rattles.
He shakes it, holds it up to a puzzled ear,
And re-opens the flap. And allows
The snake, still rattling, to slither out.

Now he pretends to be scared, he backs off
And the snake is rearing, rattling on the table
With the box on the floor, the flap
Left gaping. This lasts until the snake
Is complaisant, to be patted on the head,

But all the same it will not re-enter the box,
Which now the performer picks up with much
Less flourish than before, and closes it.
With a shake, it starts announcing, like
A transistor agreeing to work if you give it a knock.

Yes, it suddenly begins enunciating
Blatant commands: Phone us with your credit card,
Be healthy by paying for our particular
Brand of expensive health, equip your home
And your mind with my encyclopaedic sink.

It will not stop announcing, lifting the flap
Only seems to increase its volume, when closed
It only makes tenser, more bitter, more bullying statements.
So better to open all the sides of the box,
And flatten it out again, the voice

Dies out in a slur of pitiable resentment,
The performer looks at the sheet, his pretences
Not being pretences, he will not try again.
He gives a bow, for having done things, yes,
But not the things he imagined. And his smile

Is a man's outfaced by very odd events,
A man's overtaken by other performances which
Existed in the confines and the depths
Of the box somewhere, or in the air, or just
Existed like him. Performed by subtler men.

Cure

The rash fading out fades in
This annealed body, a photoprint
Coming solidly and slowly into focus
Out of a hot pink haze. Therefore a man
Is walking towards you into his daytime

And stopping, in bright mid-stride. By now
He has sharpened into something utterly
Steady, in a self-knowledge: that the scare
May never return today to re-possess
His sunlight. He is free of his own mists.

Next Meeting

A man once feared death so much he would not
Envisage it. So far away it lay,
Over successive ranges of foreign hills
In a perhaps lunar landscape, a blue
Dustbowl of inactivity and guilt.

Therefore he worked very hard, and worked
Very hard at not knowing about death,
Though all the time he was crossing seas and ridges,
Negotiating inlets and crevasses at
The breakfast table and in the Committee Room.

So meanwhile the green land was slipping back,
And his head was already above the tree-line,
He had entered a different region. He had dreamed
All his teens about an unguessed beautiful
Sleeve of the sea in the next street of his home town,

But was suddenly now at the very centre
Of his most waterless land, in a dryness
Like a blank sheet from the photocopier.
And now he was there he had no time at all
To get in all the fearing and protesting

That needed almost a lifetime. He had
The next day to think of, another agenda,
And a new pair of spectacles to see the pockmarks
On the shrivelled earth. He left a message to be called,
Set the alarm, left his papers ready,

Tapped his pillow six times about an hour before he died.

You Ask

What do I want? What is it I want to do?
– I should like to have, at an invisible quay,
At a tangent to any moral problem,
A bloody great boat, equipped with everything,
And with one operatic step, leap aboard, and leave
The rest of you behind with your confusions,
And glide away into a singing distance
Where everything is wonderfully resolved . . .

And then, one unexpected day, sail back
With another persona, yes, like someone
Else altogether, and nothing like myself,
As an unknown *deus ex machina*, making
Everyone stop and listen and behave,
Striking clarity into your souls at last, at last!
– And then pull off my mask and sing it out:
It was me! It was me! This is what I had to do!

Suspicion

She was terrified at the green shine of the sea
Between the planks of the pier,

So she held the stick hard and gnashed its crimson cloud
That fuzzed like a head of hair.

The brightness fell too soon, and the circling horses
Reared up as The Band Played On

With eyes of terror also, but painted like that,
While the girl shook on the dread

-fully quivering pier . . . And the only other
Thing she could find was a steel

Arm on a big, square, lit machine, she grabbed at it
And clanged it down. It went with

A lunge and a clatter that sent a row of discs
Insensately whirling; then

They slowed, and fixed her two passion fruit and a skull,
Which satisfied her for now.

When she turned away, the sunlight seemed perfectly
Natural, the coast restored

To an easy glistening, and the sea below
Was back to a friendly flop

-ping at the stanchions of the pier. She could breathe once more,
And gave out a little smile

As the gaps in the planks closed up. And no such thing
Would scare her again, for hours.

Through Binoculars

Between forgetting one hypochondria
And registering the next, there comes
An interval of an hour or two called *Health*,
When the world leaps into clarity and enter
A yacht, for example, over from left to right,
Red sails in the sunshine, and down there a family
With eight bright globes shaken out of a portable rack
For a game of *boule* on the beach, or I veer across
To a distant bearded man of sixty plus
Who gets a nymphet, honestly, nuzzling his forearm
– And no relation! (He will not curse if the wind
Sweeps his windbreak down.) In other words,

Short of censoriousness or pure despair,
There comes a sunnier spell called *Tolerance*,
Where I share, on this luminous oval afternoon,
The painter's way with a single shaft of light
Down on details which have shaken out themselves
Into patterns I might even see as *Hope*.
Now he stands, only a nose's length away,
The solicitor, dumping a weekend anorak
To race his green ball to the water's edge,
So his labrador, pacing him, has no need
To taste the sting of salt retrieving it.
I feel virtually happy enough to speak.

Politics

Lighting the cigarettes I need not have smoked,
I almost burnt my beard; but also found
My eyes went squinting down towards the flame,
And the page, or face, or room on the farther side
Slid out of focus into broken halves.
That was my fault entirely; but is it mine
If that girl with the Abbey National plastic bag
Is standing there, on a strip of grass between
Dual carriageways? She is ruining
My focus of this scene as a unified
View of pollution where, on the farther side,
One car in two is a speeding panda
With its blue nipple flashing to smash the pickets.

I fix my attention on the alarming Law:
The girl is on its side by standing there;
She puts an unconscious flaw and distraction
In front of my perceptions – am I to blame
If she's rather too attractive for the view?
Old men may want their youth back, but old nations
Pine for the liberties of middle-age,
The mortgage paid off, the authority . . .
In Baker Street, Sherlock Holmes smoked a pipe,
Which keeps the flame much farther from the face.
Will someone please guide that girl to safety
And clear my field of vision, before the smoke
Rolls down my throat and blinds the eyes with fears?

Scene from the Fifties

The three-year-old who will not go to bed
Tugs Gunga's tail, and Gunga patiently
Permits him to, because he understands.
An animal *knows* when it is children.

Eight o'clock now, in the drawing room
Of a house of proconsular maxims, built
In Hampshire in memory of the hills;
The lights of the town could be any town's.

She can no longer see to write, or hear
To think, so the elderly lady
Turns on the light above the wicker chair,
And licks her letter down, and turns to watch.

Watching her grandchild and the darkening fields,
She thinks, *He knows, he knows*: inside the cat
Is a small child psychotherapist resolving
To stay where he is; it makes things easier.

The mould of things seems perfectly secure:
The animals can tell when it is men;
The old man in the bedroom winds up the clock
Which tells him what time it is in Simla;

The daughter in the kitchen daintily
Prepares an England to receive them all;
The pile of 45s in Mary's room
Is not seen as something doing any harm.

In the Connecting Room

Releasing the door into its frame and facing the dark,
With the hope that the light carried forward on the eyes
Will shine through this foretaste of the absolute black . . .

And yes of course, at first an illuminating image
Is taken on from the light in the previous room
Where you sat reading, and appears to send you safely

To the door of a new one where voices and laughter
Still weave, at this moment, without interruption across
The breach about to be caused by your arrival

– Except that this pulsing beam soon diffuses
As a mazy stain spread over the pitch, and fades
To a uniform absence of light or guidance

Which no one and nothing ever countermands
Or shines a helping torch through. All that you have
Is a memory on the surface of the eye,

And after a while of this you begin to know
That you move with as little knowledge eyes closed or open,
And you might as well go groping for the artificial

Lights which are no longer there. All you could keep
Is the pictures from as many previous rooms
As you can, as long as you can. You might even hold

The print of the book you were engrossed in,
As you think it through from brain to retina.
And even the shine of music along the ear.

Devices

'. . . this cheating device of buying and selling.'
— G. Winstanley

Not having else to do, the boss strolls out
From behind his dark glass panel to keep an eye
On things in general. That hulking lout
Of an assistant has been told to see
What the customer says that they should rectify
On his electric typewriter – which he
Maintains has never functioned. Can they deny
The small print in his small green guarantee?

The boss is sighing, though it could be fuming.
Will this bugger get *something* right today!
Can he *tell* when someone thinks they'll try to swing
Repairs for their own misuse? This bloody fool
Might let a slippery customer get away
With murder . . . Has he learnt to spot the cool
Attempt to pull a fast one? Will he say
'You have not read this clause. Or kept this rule.'?

You don't *have* to be mad to work here, but
It helps – to stanch the bleeding misery;
Helps to allay the darkness of the pit
Carved in you by mad customers with lies
And surly tempers; helps calm the agony
Of sour resentment in the ferret eyes
Which turn as the boss crawls surreptitiously
Out from his hole, to fume and supervise.

Street Incident

It takes only three to look the same way
And you have an Incident. If I look as well,
That makes a fourth and Something Has Happened,
An ambulance jumps the lights and the Police
Belt out of white vans howling down our ears
Like clods of curdled metal; for nothing more
Than four people chancing suddenly to turn
At the sight of a girl's hair spiking out of
Her head like a surly palm tree.

                              But then the streets
Are filled with randomness, what happens there
Seems always sudden and deplorable.
Walking the streets I see too easily
A confluence of the worst in us, beyond
Arranging into calm or tenderness.
The streets are only there to hurry through;
Although, as I turn away, an art student looks
At a hoarding framing the scene and says, 'That's great!'
'That's aesthetic!'

                        His camera is out,
And two days later he stands up holding
A transparency to the light, the world improved
In his celluloid frame. He smiles at it, he sees
The misery transfigured, here they are,
The hoarding, the ambulance, the Police, and the palms
On the head of the passing girl, all now arranged
Into one aesthetic greatness; and there is nothing
Less like a question in his shining eyes.

Fire Drill

Now we all troop out, now we all troop out
Along the arrows on the notices;

But it's not for real, they told us in advance
There was going to be an exercise.

The hooter blares on down long corridors
And over into portakabins. Here

Is a word half-finished on a typewriter,
There, a comb stopped in half-done hair. Miss West,

Never seen full-length before, is standing up
And out from behind her desk, Mr Vince

Hasn't rescued the word-processor from the flames,
But he has saved some important-looking memos.

What would we do, we say, if it were true,
And not a practice! Leaving our coats inside,

We pour out, as instructed, from the main doors
And the side doors; and all protocol has gone.

On the equal grass today's warm sun and breeze
Flow round our unusual outdoor laughter,

And anyone talks to anyone. Back inside,
In the empty spaces, nothing can be the same.

We shall go back with a sense of changing,
To rooms where the sun falls in a different place.

– But we can't go back, they want a photograph.
They want a photograph and had not told us.

Stand still – like that – stand still, *stand still!*
There is going to be a tremendous flash.

The Boyhood of Raleigh

But the end of it all was a shuffling line of ten thousand
Stretched out at the airport, everyone in search
Of a difference not too discomposing:
A compatible sort of bathing, docile fauna
Trotting up to nuzzle on the hotel steps,
A wheel of chance where every player wins . . .
'And when we were there it felt easy to be there,
And now we are back it feels truthful to say
"I don't feel I'm back" or "I don't feel I ever went",
The place was an illusion. We were not illusions ourselves,
We made the links between what you call "different" places,
Which are more the same because we have left our impression,
Which modifies the place as one wave modifies a beach,
Or "like" another English changes your own.
We sit with the arm of our traveller's tale extended,
Reciting the fictions of distance, we tip up our bags
And find the fool's gold of unchangeable coins,
The centimes, the bani, and here in the bottom
An unused token for a locker in Central Station,
We'll use it next time. And the children are amazed,
The boys want to go when they are adults, or when they have
   passports,
They have sat long enough being just themselves
On this side of the sea, can't they be it on the other side as well?
"Look at this!" they would like to say, holding up
The plunders of the gift shop. "You see, you see!
It proves we have been there and thought of you.
We weren't alarmed by the difference at all.
It was so immense we have brought back part of it
To be found nowhere else but there (and Victoria Station):
A Duty Free ballpoint pen with a toucan's head!"'

What one boy thought and wrote in the room beyond
The gift shop and the green channel was
A distant recollection, of himself. All his words
Lay silent in the books, the forests continued
To grow without him, and the plundered chests of coins
Closed their lids as if he had never brought any back.
The wheel had turned and turned and stopped there.
He had gone no farther than his heart had sent him
On its regular missions of circulation.

The Rain Diary

For my geography project I would keep a rain diary, a record starting on 1st January of the days that year when it rained and approximately how much.

On 1st January there was no rain. On 2nd January there was no rain. It did not rain on 3rd or 4th either. Would I go back to school on 8th January with nothing to show? Only blank pages with the dates in blue-black italic and the expectation of punishment?

Amanda kept a sunshine diary. The sun shone all the time that New Year, every day was like the legendary 1st January 1942. I saw long shadows of bare trees in Amanda's garden revolving on the stiff white grass as the sun crawled low and bright round the Warwickshire sky. Amanda, day by day, logged her hours of sunshine in duffle coat and mittens, putting out her tongue to warm her finger tips.

Tiny planes inched over the blue from the aerodrome leaving lacy strips of vapour which crumbled into strung-out blurs. There was no rain on 5th, 6th or 7th. I gained a sense of what life in general would be like.

On 8th January I stood at 8.55 a.m. on the worn stone step of the school with my blank diary – and raindrops fell. But I had no time to write anything down, the bell was pounding in the school campanile and we could not be late. So I opened my rain diary and let the rain fall into it, stain it and crinkle it, as the others fled past me into school.

To which rain I added my own joyful tears, knowing that Amanda might have statistics but I had a concrete event.

Leading Down

Can you see it, in the distance? It is preparing
To arrive soon, that white wave breaking
On some shoal of your hidden self. It's wearing
Life's one undoubted crown, your special fear
Confirmed now. And that sight will greet you
Many times more with each remaining year,
On any shore of sleep, or strand of waking.
– Far inland too, it will be there to greet you.

And it's coming whenever you look. Even he who dreads
To glance out there at all, at the very last
Will recognise it when it drops and spreads
In colourless ripples at his own feet
– Then rises suddenly. For each of the many
Times it withdrew, it has come back to repeat
His particular message; and risen to share its fast
And final secret, not held back from any.

We listen when others say it's getting nearer,
And nod at their anxiety. We are so strong
We need not dread it yet. We have a clearer
View of it while it still stays well away.
We can commiserate, and with our pity
Patronise the dead. To ourselves we say
We do not feel we need begin the long
Appraisal of our own mortality.

But here, in deep and crowded quiet, we sense
How your wave returned, for you; and every face
Stares emptily out there, in an intense
Rehearsal of its doubt.
                   The daylight fades.
I drive the streets leading down to your slow
Wide estuary, where all day's lively shades
Are one bleak dark. The tide has ebbed a space;
And I am sure only that it will flow.